To Marion ~

beloved sister
and best friend ~

You have fought the good fight
you have finished your course
you have kept the faith.

Rest in peace...
...till we meet again.

Salesian Missions wishes to extend special thanks and gratitude to our generous poet friends and to the publishers who have given us permission to reprint material included in this book. Every effort has been made to give proper acknowledgments. Any omissions or errors are deeply regretted, and the publisher, upon notification, will be pleased to make the necessary corrections in subsequent editions.

Pathways of Life

from the
Salesian Collection

Compiled and Edited
by Sara Tarascio

Illustrated by
Paul Scully,
Frank Massa
and
Russell Bushée

CONTENTS

So swiftly run the sands of time

So carelessly we scatter

Its rare and precious golden grains

On things that do not matter...

Helen Courcier

Sand

I think of the sand on the beach
with millions of grains in my hand,
and wonder how much the Lord placed
on beaches all through the land.

I think of the millions of people
scattered all over the earth,
comparing each one to a grain,
and each with a purpose for birth.

God's wonders surround us each day.
Such splendor only God could create,
and only a fool could deny
a wisdom and glory so great.

And just like the sand on the beach,
each person is ever so small.
But God's grace is always sufficient.
God nurtures and cares for us all.

Edna Massimilla

A Time of Retreat

We cannot find contentment
    Nor can life be complete;
Unless we take some time each day
    To rest at Jesus' feet.

To find a quiet corner
    Where we can go to Him;
Who is our precious Prince of Peace
    Whose peace begins within.

Just think of quiet meadows
    A church with ringing bell;
Which is the only sound we hear
    Within a country dell.

But hamlet or a city
    Wherever we may be;
A quiet time with Christ each day
    Restores Serenity.

So let us seek our Saviour
    On each and every day;
So He can bless us through His Love
    In His own precious way!

Sancie Earman King

We Call It "Home"

There is someone who truly cares for us,
Who knows each thought and hears each word we say,
Our Friend, not just when things are going great,
But through the times we fall along the way.
There is Someone on whom we can depend,
Who also walked the crooked paths we trod,
Who knows our joy, and understands our pain,
. . . We call Him God.

There is a mighty force that rules the earth,
Its' presence even makes the bitter, sweet,
It must abide in every heart before
Any man can say his life's complete.
It can transcend the very blackest night,
And like the dazzling sunlight from above,
It warms and strengthens that on which it falls,
. . . We call it love.

There is a place which we've been told about,
A heaven that no mortal eye can see,
A promised refuge at the journey's end,
To be with God for all eternity.
Where we shall meet our loved ones gone before,
Find blessed peace, no more to ever roam,
With nevermore a sorrow or a sigh,
. . . We call it home.

Grace E. Easley

For My Home

Dear Lord, I thank You for my home,
For these four walls to call my own
Where in life's solitude and rest
I am with those I love the best.
I thank You for their love as well
That makes it possible to dwell
In peace and comfort such as ours.
I thank You for the fragrant flowers
That bloom the whole long summer through
And for the rain and sunshine, too,
And friends and neighbors on our street.
I thank You Lord, for life complete.

Edna Pinkerton Hirons

10

Simple Things

I'm thankful for the simple things
    in life that mean so much -
Like a small hand slipping into mine,
    or a kitten's friendly touch...

Like the sound of raindrops falling
    on my roof at 2 A.M.;
Or the song a bird is singing,
    perched upon an old oak limb...

Simple things like fragrant flowers
    blooming just outside my door;
Or the smell of clean, fresh pine scent
    coming from Mom's kitchen floor...

Like the taste of home-fried chicken
    like my grandma use to make;
Or that first-poured cup of coffee
    that helps sleepy eyes awake...

Simple things like seasons changing -
    winter, spring, then summer and fall;
Or the colors in a rainbow -
    Lord, there's beauty in it all.

May I never take for granted
    all of life's "simplicities,"
For they're gifts You chose to give me
    to fill all my memories.

                Diana Sue Lindley

Flowers of May

April left the gate ajar,
   And May skipped boldly in;
Led by hordes of daffodils,
   With all their golden kin.

Early roses came along,
   And climbed the garden wall,
Followed by scarlet tulips -
   The gayest of them all.

Trim pansies in their turn,
   Sprang from sun-kissed sod,
And had their tiny faces washed
   With dewdrops sent by God.

May days now soon must end -
   Although they seem so few.
June is waiting in the wings,
   And lovely May must bid adieu.

Erma Fajen MacFarlane

Little Favors

Thank You, Lord, for little favors
That You do for me each day
And for little gifts and blessings
That You shower upon my ways.
They are, always, rich endearments
That add comfort to my life
And a strength of heart and courage
To endure the woes of strife.

They are, seldom, gifts of greatness -
That You grace on holy souls -
Or the special kind of blessings
You reward for Christian goals -
They're just, simply, little favors
That You do for me each day
To remind me that You love me
And are never far away.

Michael Dubina

Introspection

I hold no dreams of fortune vast
    Nor seek undying fame.
I do not ask when life is past
    That many know my name.

I may not own the skill to rise
    To glories topmost height
Nor win a place among the wise
    But I can keep the right.

And I can live my life on earth
    Contented to the end
If but a few shall know my worth
    And proudly call me friend.

I like to think when life is done
    That I had filled a needed post
That here and there, I'd paid my fare
    With more than idle talk and boast.

That I had taken gifts Divine
    The breath of life and talents fine,
And tried to use them now and then
    In service to my fellow men.

Mildred Beebe

Love Makes
Everything Beautiful

Love makes everything beautiful
    to those who seek her face.
Behind the veil of fear and doubt
    she offers peace and grace.

Love keeps a bedside vigil
    throughout the lonely night,
And holds the gnarled, dying hand
    that reaches for the light.

Love rocks the midnight cradle
    and whispers lullabies...
It cleans the house, mends our clothes
    and bakes us apple pies.

Love takes the time to listen
    to a beggar's fond request,
And lifts grateful eyes to Heaven
    when a bird leaves its nest.

Love never takes for granted
    the Master's wondrous grace...
Love makes everything beautiful
    to those who seek her face.

Clay Harrison

Our Faith in God

We've had our "ups and downs" in life,
Our "ups" were mighty few,
Our "downs" it seems were many,
But we always did pull through.
When "bad spells" seemed to hit us,
And the road was hard to trod,
We always pulled together,
And put our Faith in God.

We always seemed to make it
When the going was real tough,
At times I really had my doubts,
And nearly "had enough."
But, we all stuck together,
Like "peas within a pod,"
We buckled down, and won, because
We put "Our Faith in God."

Bill Carr

December

When December drops his mantle,
Then all around the region;
We find ourselves confronted by,
King Winter's hoary legions.

And as the days get colder,
And the snow begins to fall;
We realize Autumn's over,
And we soon will have some squalls.

The streams start getting glassy,
And the north wind fiercely blows
And anytime we go outside,
We freeze our nose, and toes.

But then life starts to brighten,
As the bells of Christmas ring;
And all around the city;
We can hear the carolers sing.

And we find out that truly,
It's a great time to be living;
For this is when the world breaks out,
With loving, and with giving.

But then December slips away
I quietly shed a tear.
For this not only ends a month;
It's the night-fall of a year.

Wesley Yonts

The Wise
Old Owl

Like the Solomon of fowl
Sat a wise old owl
Perched in a sycamore tree,
While the moonlight glimmered
And the starlight shimmered,
These words he spoke to me:

"I guess you've heard
I'm a wise old bird,
And if wisdom you would find...
Always look for the best
And your life will be blest,
To all others' faults be blind.

In this life, I know
You will find it so
That if you think kindly of others,
You'll soon find that it's true
They'll think kindly of you...
Praise your sisters and your brothers!"

You may think me a fool -
Owls don't talk, as a rule,
But in solemn tone, he said:
"Don't be quick to enact
Words you'll wish to retract,
Dwell upon the good instead!"

Though I hate to admit it,
I could see, once I did it
What that wise owl said was true.
Your faults I'll overlook
'Cause it says in the book
What you sow comes back to you!

Now, if you will agree
With what he said to me,
Then my faults you will ignore...
Like that sage bird said
We'll both come out ahead
If we judge less and praise more!

Connie Hinnen

An Old
Fashioned Winter

As children, we would gather 'round
The hearthfire and its cheerful glow
And listen to the crackling sound
Of burning logs, with lamps turned low.
We'd gaze wide-eyed into the fire
Delaying when we had to go
To chilly bedrooms to retire,
When trying to keep warm was our
    one main desire.

But in our featherbeds so light,
With hot wrapped irons at our feet,
We'd sleep all through the blustery night,
Oblivious of the snow and sleet.
At daybreak, when the sun would peep
Through shuttered window old and worn,
Out of our cozy beds we'd creep
To view the scene left by the storm
And find a glistening landscape strewn
With branches torn.

      Elsie Natalie Brady

Keep on Going...

Don't let this old world get you down
When you are sad and blue;
Ignore the clouds that fill the sky,
And let the sun shine through,
And keep on going...

Don't let this old world get you down
When you have need to cry--
Just dry those tears and you will see
A rainbow in the sky,
And keep on going...

Don't let this old world get you down
When things don't turn out right;
A new day soon will dawn for you,
And chase away the night,
So keep on going...

Don't let this old world get you down
When you are touched by woe;
The Lord will take you by the hand
Because He loves you so;
Just keep on going!

Hope C. Oberhelman

*L*ike a bird
singing in the rain,
let grateful memories
survive in time of sorrow.

Robert Louis Stevenson

Mine, The World

Mine the world... each blessed inch of it,
Inherited since first the world began.
I need no deed to show my ownership,
It's written on the heart of every man!
Mine the grey chiffon of autumn mist,
The virgin blush that dawn can never hide,
The burnished copper sunset streaked with gold,
The muted sonnets whispered by the tide!

Translucent twilight steeped in perfume of
The honeysuckle thick upon the walls;
The quiet woodland, lush with lacy fern,
On which the dappled sunlight softly falls...
Mine the rain in slanted silver lines,
The velvet fog on quiet little feet,
And as the hours slowly trickle by,
Affinity with nature's great heartbeat!

Mine the world that stretches far and wide,
The rainbow's arc above a distant hill,
The sight of scarlet red-bud through the brush,
The echo of a plaintive whippoorwill!
Humble am I before the majesty,
Of fragile little buttercups unfurled.
Greater than mine, no wealth has any man...
For mine... the world!

Grace E. Easley

My Walk with God

When my busy week has ended
To the country I will trod
Just to feel the closeness of Him
As I take my walk with God.

Hand in hand from hill to valley
Sweet the smell of fresh turned sod
Sweeter still my joy and pleasure
As I take my walk with God.

Every creature pays Him homage
Trees and flowers bow and nod
In the presence of their maker
As I take my walk with God.

Oh the rapture of this moment
Guided by His staff and rod
Lifted now are all my burdens
As I take my walk with God.

                    Albert N. Theel

Contemplation
on a
Morning Walk

He smiles at me in the rising sun,
　　He sings in every bird,
As the wind flutters leaves, one by one,
　　His silent voice is heard.

His gentle hand holds the opening flower,
　　And spreads the petals wide,
All evidence of creation power,
　　Is in a place where pansies hide.

He provides the deer that delights my eye,
　　The squirrel that climbs a tree,
And snails that slither as I pass by,
　　He gave them all to me.

He is found in quiet contemplation,
　　Wordless - Yet I hear Him talk,
He is known in ever deeper measure,
　　All in a morning walk.

Betty Dobrowolski

Thank You, God, for This Day

This was the friendliest day,
There were smiles all along the way;
There were "How-do-you-do's"
Coming out of the blue...
O, this was the friendliest day.

This was the happiest day,
There were flowers strewn along the way.
Flowers of sweet words
Were all that I heard...
O, this was the happiest day.

This was a velvet-wrapped day,
Ribboned with bright sunny rays.
Right from the start joy filled my heart...
Thank You, God, for this day.

Loise Pinkerton Fritz

Puppy Love

The night was cold, so bitter cold,
And snow lay on the ground,
I heard a weak and piteous whine,
A muffled, scratching sound.

I looked outside, and I could see,
A tiny puppy there,
Huddled in a shivering heap
Of whitely-frosted hair.

Someone's abandoned you, I thought,
Someone who didn't care,
Unloved, unwanted, cast aside,
To me, it seemed unfair.

I looked into his soft brown eyes,
My own eyes filled with tears,
I made my lonely heart his home,
To share down through the years.

I watched him run and play and grow,
Through happy days we shared,
I'd found a friend who needed me,
He'd found a friend who cared.

Julie E. Jones

Sounds of Spring

From where I sit beside the lake
God's creatures seem to come awake
The time of singing birds is come
The winter season overcome.

The whistling sound of wind in the tree
The flashing colors of birds flying free
The buzzing of bees and butterflies
Mother Nature's way to harmonize.

Earth comes to life freshly renewed
A new growing season of life anew
She has her way of bringing cheer
And telling us God is very near.

Hush - and listen to the sounds of Spring
The sound of the wind; the bird on wing;
Warmth of the sun; the patter of rain
Mother Nature's change-of-seasons plain.

Toby Munson

When Summer Comes

The mountain stream awakens now
    As late Spring's ice and snow
No longer hold her where she is
    But slowly let her go.

And singing down the mountain side
    She dances through the day
Past sunny banks of green and gold
    For Summer's on the way.

The great black bear surveys the hills
    Hawks sail the endless skies,
The flowers blush across the fields
    To tempt the butterflies.

And through the trees the Summer breeze
    Does whisper as she goes,
"Blest be the hand that made this land
    And everything that grows."

"The gentle hand that made the rose
    So velvet soft and mild,
The mighty hand that made these hills
    So beautiful and wild!"

Kate Watkins Furman

Simple Joys

Oh, give me the simple joys
That truly make life sweet,
Home and hearth and loved ones,
A pet beside one's feet...
The sound of lovely music,
A cup of fragrant tea,
A walk through primrose paths
In a greening country lea...
A good book at the bedside,
A friend that's ever true,
The warming days of summer,
The Autumn's vibrant view...
Oh, give me the simple joys,
And I'll not ask for more
For in them lies great happiness,
Within and by my door.

Virginia Borman Grimmer

My Garden

I planted a little garden
　　One early sunny morn.
Lettuce, tomatoes, cabbage, beets,
　　Pickles, carrots, corn.
The sun and rain soon made them grow,
　　And show their leaves of green.
I watered my garden carefully,
　　Kept it neat and clean.

'Twas a lovely little garden,
　　But as summer days drew near,
I forgot my little garden,
　　Thought it needed no more care.
As days went by my garden grew,
　　For I had sown the seeds,
But this I could not understand,
　　Who has sown the weeds?

For they had grown much faster
　　Than the seeds that I had sown;
And the lettuce, tomatoes, cabbage, beets,
　　Pickles, carrots, corn,
Had never had a chance to grow
　　To full maturity;
Because I hadn't pulled the weeds,
　　That, I could plainly see.

And so 'tis with this heart of mine,
　　The good seeds soon will grow.
But evil seeds are sown there, too,
　　And this one thing I know;
Daily, I must keep it clean,
　　And let the good seeds grow,
Till all my heart is free from weeds,
　　With Heaven's light aglow.

Helen Humbarger

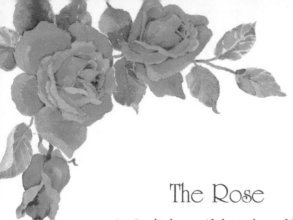

The Rose

In God's beautiful garden of flowers,
The touch of His hand is so clear,
And I know when I look at each blossom,
He is telling me that He is near.

There are flowers of strength and of stature,
There are some that speak peace and repose,
But none touches my heart when I see it,
Like the beautiful, delicate rose.

The petals are soft and so fragrant,
And if left in God's hand to unfold,
They will perfectly form such a blossom,
That is joy for the eye to behold.

But if I take that rosebud in my hand,
And open its petals my way,
I quickly can see that the flower I formed,
Can't compare to His wonderous display.

God has graciously taught me a lesson,
And by using the rose made me see,
That I, like this delicate flower,
Must let Him unfold my life for me.

Shirley M. Jones

Faith is a Rose

Faith is a rose that blooms
   within the human heart
To glorify God's garden
   where men are set apart.

In spring the buds are bursting
   with radiance anew
Petals tightly closed in prayer
   bathed in the morning dew.

As the Master tends His garden,
   the petals open wide
To magnify and praise Him
   throughout the countryside.

Then come the winds of autumn
   and soon the petals fall,
But fond memories remain
   as snowflakes come to call.

For once again in spring
   the rose shall bloom anew
Within the Master's garden
   where other roses grew.

Clay Harrison

Wayward Heart

I've lived with angers, hates and scorns
   Throughout my wayward life
And searched for love - where love despairs -
   In bowers of sinful strife;
And God was never friend to me -
   To ban my wayward ways -
For I was tyrant to His laws
   And rebel to obey.

I never prayed to Him for help -
   To rid my life of hates -
And never sought His touch of Grace
   To balm my tearful fates.
I walked alone - with angry heart -
   And lived each new born day
Without a purpose or a goal -
   Or cause to change my ways.

But, now, has come a time of truth -
    When past and future meet -
And I must separate the truths
    From years of self deceit
For, now, my burdens are too great
    For me, alone, to bear -
I must implore the help of God
    To lift me from despair.

And I must seek His love and Grace
    To help me change my ways,
And change my thoughts and wills of mind
    That darken all my days
For I cannot continue so -
    With wayward heart of sins -
I must resign my life to God
    And place my trust in Him.

           Michael Dubina

The Light Above

When our eyes have lost the wonder
  Of earth's beauty that is rare,
And our hearts have lost all feeling
  Dark depression everywhere.

When we hear no songs of beauty
  And we feel so all alone,
As we walk a lonely pathway
  With a heart as cold as stone.

In this lonely vale of sorrow
  If we only look above,
We can see the Greatest Wonder
  Is the wonder of God's love.

For in every cold dark valley
  We can see a light above,
Even in the vale of teardrops
  We are walking in His love.

If we only seek our Savior
  And we seek the light above,
He will bear us up the mountain
  In the wonder of His love.

Gertrude B. McClain

God
Loveth Me

Sometimes I get to thinking
Of the way You care for me,
And I feel so very humble,
That such a thing could be.
For I'm only just a creature
That You fashioned out of clay,
But You're always making sure that I
Have all I need each day.

Sometimes when I am worried,
And I don't know what to do,
And things don't seem to work out,
I always run to You.
And what I thought were problems,
Vanish 'neath Your hand,
You take the time to listen,
And You always understand.

My dwelling may be humble,
But You share my small abode,
And when I feel I'm sinking,
You are there to lift the load.
And I count myself the luckiest,
That anyone can be,
Because I know beyond a doubt,
…My Savior loveth me!

Grace E. Easley

A Friendly Smile

Don't tell your troubles to the world.
We all have loads to bear.
You can remove a lot of them
By kneeling down in prayer.
Then find a goodly deed to do.
It won't be very long
Until that grumbling me, oh my,
Is changed into a song.
A loving personality
Is such a special treat;
A friendly smile can lift the cares
Of people that you meet.
God put His rainbow in the clouds
For beauty after gray,
So put a rainbow in your heart,
And have a happy day.

Norma Childress

Pilgrim's Progress

Each time I face decisions, Lord,
    and wonder what to do
about some choices I must make,
    I leave them up to You.

I'll think of plus and minuses
    till every choice seems right
and try too long to think things through
    without Your guiding light.

It's never matter of what's right
    or good or best for me;
I know I must fulfill Your will
    however that may be.

Although life, then, becomes too hard
    and full of problems, too,
it's only when I choose Your way
    I show true love for You.

             Eugene G. E. Botelho

*P*raise to Thee, my Lord,
for all Thy creatures...

St. Francis of Assisi

A Daily Prayer

Dear God, I ask forgiveness
For all the wrong I do.
I know I am not worthy
Of love bestowed by You.
You strengthen and sustain me
In time of my despair.
You give me hope and courage
In answer to my prayer.
I know I am not perfect
And cannot hope to be,
But with Your great compassion
I know that You love me.
I thank You God with humble heart
For all You give and do.
There is no day that e'er goes by
I do not kneel to You.

Harold F. Mohn

A Thankful Morning

Another day has dawned, Lord.
Its beauty is mine to see;
And this morning I give thanks to You
For watching over me.

For last night while I slept, Lord,
You kept me in Your care;
Protected me and saved me
From dangers unaware.

I fell asleep, my mind at ease,
Just knowing You would be
In constant vigil by my side,
Til darkened hours would flee.

So as I enter this new day
You've brought me safely to,
It's my desire to live it
In a way that pleases You.

Diana Sue Lindley

*"I laid me down and slept;
I awaked; for the Lord
sustained me.*
Psalm 3:5

Eloquence of God

He speaks to us in song of birds
In trees where birds can build a nest,
The roaring tide, the quiet breeze,
The meadow with its wild flowers blest.

He speaks to us at close of day
With sunset's every wondrous hue;
The brilliant gold and amber tone,
The silver shade, the mauve, the blue.

He speaks to us in harvest field
In waves of ripening, golden grain;
He gives a benediction prayer
In sun and shadow, wind and rain.

He offers us four season times
In winter, summer, autumn, spring;
If we would only listen well,
God speaks to us in everything.

Juanita R. Davis

Wintertime

The moonlight on the snow of white
Was lovely in the still of night,
And shadows soft were lingering there
Beneath the sky so wondrous fair,
The winter air was crisp and cold
The winter night so fresh and bold,
And yet the world seemed safe and sure
Enfolded in a dream secure.

A million stars were looking down
Upon each friendly lighted town,
On country roads the snow piled high
To thrill each little passer-by,
For children marvelled at the snow
And really loved the winter so,
Their laughter warmed the chilling night
And everywhere the world was white.

Bright wintertime, oh what a thrill
With sledding on the far off hill,
The valley smiling far below
A shelter from the cold and snow,
God's world became a rich delight
When winter decked it all in white,
A treasured magic, yours and mine
This wondrous, glorious wintertime.

Garnett Ann Schultz

In Evening's Peace

Blue twilight, soft as angels' wings
    Has swept old Winter's sky,
Where icy winds slipped through the trees
    And sought the mountains high.
From one small home one shining light
    Illuminates the snow,
Where burns the warmth of love and fire
    As evening's shadows grow.
The smoke ascends the silvered sky
    A pure and silent prayer,
That begs the holy grace of God
    For all assembled there.
And peace, sweet peace; oh, blessed peace,
    It's you that here we find,
Upon the land, upon the house
    Upon the heart and mind.

                  Kate Watkins Furman

Precious Moments

Ah, the Precious Moments
That keep us day to day
The little things that touch our hearts
That others do and say.

The look upon a baby's face
Asleep in Mother's arms
A kitten rolling 'cross the floor
With Gramma's ball of yarn.

The picture that a child paints
Seen only through their eyes
In hopes that when they bring it home
Mom will smile with surprise.

A phone call from a dear friend
When somehow, they just know
That you are feeling blue today
Just in time... their love... they show.

A flower from your husband
Or dinner on the table
When you were wondering what to fix
Or if you would be able.

Yes, I thank God for Precious Moments
That keep us day to day
The little things that touch our hearts
That others do and say.

Debbie Immel North

Your Dog

Your dog may have a pedigree
As far as records reach,
And it may be obedient
To everything you teach,
Or it may be a common mutt
That lingers at your feet,
Because somewhere it found you, as
You walked along the street.
It may become a champion
Or just a household pet,
But if you love that animal
It never will forget.
For every pat you give it, and
For every friendly smile,
Your dog will cuddle up to you
And follow you each mile.
It will be truly loyal, and
Protect you to the end,
Yes, it will even die for you
To prove it is your friend.

James J. Metcalfe

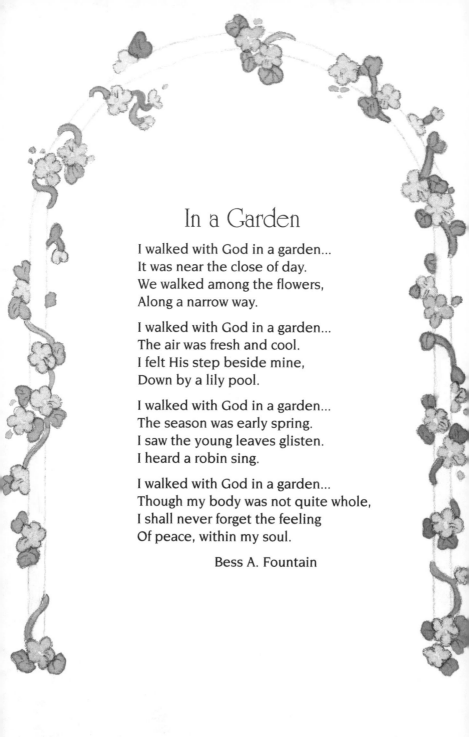

In a Garden

I walked with God in a garden...
It was near the close of day.
We walked among the flowers,
Along a narrow way.

I walked with God in a garden...
The air was fresh and cool.
I felt His step beside mine,
Down by a lily pool.

I walked with God in a garden...
The season was early spring.
I saw the young leaves glisten.
I heard a robin sing.

I walked with God in a garden...
Though my body was not quite whole,
I shall never forget the feeling
Of peace, within my soul.

Bess A. Fountain

Life is Like the Seasons

Spring and Summer, Fall and Winter,
Life is like the seasons,
Partly joy and partly sorrow,
For whatever reasons.
A time for youth, a time for age,
'Tis written in God's Plan,
And only one's allotted years,
Are granted any man.

The hour of departure,
Is hidden from our eyes,
Still we go on collecting all
That in a moment dies.
Forgetting, like the seasons,
That new replaces old,
And all that we may take with us,
...Is our immortal soul.

Grace E. Easley

Thy sunshine smiles

upon the winter days of my heart,

never doubting of its spring flowers.

Rabindranath Tagore

God Answers Prayer

Not a moment too soon
Not a moment too late
God will answer the prayer
That is offered in faith.
For if in our hearts
We truly believe
In the fullness of time
We will surely receive.

Sometimes He surprises
And answers at once,
Sometimes we must wait
For weeks, perhaps months,
But God who is faithful
Hears when we pray
And He will answer
In His own divine way.

Not always the way
We think or expect,
Not always the path
We ourselves would select,
But God in His wisdom
Knows what is best,
Oh blessed assurance,
Our souls can now rest.

Rosemary J. Tivey

*"Call unto me, and I will answer
thee, and show thee great and
mighty things."*
Jeremiah 33:3

God Loves
A Thankful Heart

Have you thanked God in the morning,
When the sun lit up the blue,
That He watched you all the nighttime
And brought you safely through
To see another day of life
In which to live for Him,
The One Who lights our pathway here
In this dark world of sin?

Have you thanked God in the evening
For each opportunity
To share the love of Jesus
Who died for you and me?
God loves a thankful heart, we know,
And one that in Him rests;
Oh, let us ever thankful be...
Then you and me He'll bless.

Loise Pinkerton Fritz

*"Give thanks always. Such is God's
will for you in Christ Jesus."*
I Thess. 5:18

Love Alone
Will Last

Though life is often full of strife,
the only thing that counts in life,
is Heaven's love that dwells within
and helps us conquer hate and sin.

Though life is often full of pain,
our lives are never lived in vain,
for though the tears may cloud the eye,
the love of God will never die.

Though kings and kingdoms all may fall,
the child is wiser than us all --
who knows that love alone will last
when all the trials of life are past.

So do not let your love depart,
for Heaven lives within your heart --
it shines its light from high above
and dwells within your heart as love.

Alvin Finkelstein

Thank You

Oh, it's so good to be living
     When the season of springtime is here;
When the flowers are once again blooming
     And the skies are less cloudy than clear.

Oh, it's so good to be living
     When the season of summer is here;
When soft, cooling breezes are blowing
     And streamlets seem saying, "come here."

Oh, it's so good to be living
     When the season of autumn is here;
When Jack Frost with his magical fingers
     Makes the tints on the foliage appear.

Oh, it's so good to be living
     When the season of winter is here;
When hearth fires are glowing a welcome
     Giving forth warmness and cheer.

Oh, but it's good to be living
     At any old time of the year;
My heart's overflowing with "thank you's"
     For the privilege of just being here.

                    Clare (Rachel) Hartnett

His Presence - The Promise

Life inspires my spirits to soar,
my soul rejoices as never before.
Joys freely flow from the morning sun,
with a faith to last until day is done.

And with the evening's peaceful rest
comes hope for the 'morrows unending quest.
For the quest is certain, the journey is clear,
to live in His image and to banish all fears.

To pause to comfort, to brighten one's day,
to patiently, prayerfully show others the way.
To share someone's burden and friendship impart,
to offer consolation to each sorrowful heart.

For God is the giver of treasures untold,
as each day the mysteries of our life unfold.
So we offer our prayers of honor and praise,
His presence the promise, till the end of our days.

Loretta Garing

Hold My Hand, Lord

Hold my hand through troubled waters,
Lord, I'm tempest-tossed and frail;
Without Thee, I'd surely flounder
Like a ship without a sail.
Be my anchor, lest I perish
For there is no help but Thee.
With Thy mighty strength, uphold me
While I cross this stormy sea.

Sorrow's clouds are growing darker;
Paths ahead, I cannot see,
And the gales blow fierce about me…
Thou, my Savior, pilot me!
What a comfort, Lord to know Thee!
Feel Thy blessed presence near;
And to hear Thee gently whisper
"Child, I'm with you… do not fear."

I accept this trial from Thee, Lord,
For I know 'tis as You've planned;
And I'll trust Thy love and wisdom
Though I do not understand.
One glad day, I'll know the reason,
See Thy blessing now disguised,
Know just why You chose to lead me
Through these waters deep and wide.

But for now… just hold my hand, Lord,
And together we will row
Through this sea of troubled waters.
'Tis enough for me to know
That You never will forsake me
In the blackness of the night;
And Your love will safely guide me
Through the storm to morning light.

                    Beverly J. Anderson

New
Beginnings

It's only the beginning now
    …a pathway yet unknown,
At times the sound of other steps
    …sometimes we walk alone.

The best beginnings of our lives
    May sometimes end in sorrow,
But even on our darkest days
    …the sun will shine tomorrow.

So we must do our very best
    Whatever life may bring,
And look beyond the winter chill
    …to smell the breath of spring.

Into each life will always come
    A time to start anew,
A new beginning for each heart
    …as fresh as morning dew.

Although the cares of life are great
    And heads are bowed so low,
The storms of life will leave behind
    …the wonder of a rainbow.

The years will never take away
    Our chance to start anew,
It's only the beginning now
    So dreams can still come true.

Gertrude B. McClain

Don't Miss the Wonder of Today

Don't miss the wonder of today.
Your heart can make a little happiness
Watching the sun put yellow diamonds
In the trees, and candles in the flowers --
Wait for the birds to sing
In silent gardens, and butterflies
To make their poems everywhere.
Even the rain will be
Your silver friend.
Even the storm that has a music all its own.
No matter where you walk
Your heart can make a dream
Of everything if God is there.
Don't miss the wonder of today!

Marion Schoeberlein

Our Source of Light

There is but one and only One
    Who conquers dusk and brings the sun;
And that is Christ, whose shining face
    Can brighten all through smile of grace.

For when the skies are dark above,
    Our woes are conquered through His love;
As only Christ, and He alone
    Can lighten every burden known.

When sorrow makes the teardrops fall,
    And darkness settles over all;
We have a Friend who's always there
    To heal our hurts through balm of prayer.

Then let us lift our hearts to Him
    That joy of life may thus begin;
Through Christ, whose presence like a balm
    Can every type of tempest calm.

For if we trust in Jesus' love.
    It makes the angels smile above;
For there can reign no more the night
    When Christ Himself is source of light!

Sancie Earman King

Winter's Coronation

Icicles overnight appear
    like prisms on a chandelier...
Winter in her gown of white
    is magnificent in moonlight!

Dawn unwraps a purple shawl,
    silver shadows slowly fall...
Silken flakes of drifting snow
    decorate the trees below.

Summer's green cannot be seen
    concealed beneath a satin sheen...
There is cause for celebration
    at Winter's annual coronation.

Clay Harrison

*Thou has set all
the borders of the
earth; Thou has
made summer
and winter.*
Ps. 74:17

Smiles of Faith

I, often, feel - my lot in life -
Is willed to be unfair
And I possess life's greatest woes
Of heartache and despair
Until, at times, I see a soul
Who suffers more than I
But wears a smile, upon his face,
That every pain denies.

I am reminded, at such times,
That I am wanting faith -
And lacking love and trust in God,
As Master of my fate;
For it is He, who lights a smile
Upon a sufferer's face;
And it is He, who blesses faith
With courage, love and Grace.

Michael Dubina

If Only I --

If only I had helped the man
    Who had no coat when I had two,
Or had I shared my blessings then
    With someone else who had but few.

If only I had taken time
    My fellow man to understand,
To bring new hope to lonely ones
    Who reach in vain for someone's hand.

Today I'll start to change the "ifs"
    Erase the words, "If only I --"
I'll give to him who needs my help
    And greet the stranger passing by.

I'll strive each day to do my best
    To heed some neighbor's urgent cry;
At close of day I'll have no need
    To speak the words, "If only I --."

Ronald Eyrich

He that hath two
coats, let him impart
to him who hath none.
Luke 3:11

63

We Thank You, God!

For life's glorious adventure,
    living in Your wondrous world,
For the solid earth beneath us,
    For the universe, unfurled,
        We thank You, God!

For beauty that our eyes behold,
    all around us everywhere,
For inner sight to understand
    ourselves and others in our care,
        We thank You, God!

For sounds of music, songs of birds,
    For human voices, sweet and clear,
    of loving family and friends,
For all of those our hearts hold dear,
        We thank You, God!

For Your still small voice within,
    Christ's loving presence, night and day,
Guiding and protecting us
    every step along life's way,
        We thank You, God!

                Micky Meyer Mathewson

Nocturnal Prayer...

Dear Father, thank Thee for Thy peace,
And for Thy blessed love;
Thank Thee for Thy faith and hope,
And guidance from above...

Dear Father, thank Thee for Thy peace,
And for Thy caring ways;
Look down on us with joy and light,
And brighten up our days...

Dear Father, thank Thee for Thy peace,
And for Thy tender care;
Come walk with us, almighty God,
And touch our lives with prayer...

Dear Father, thank Thee for Thy peace,
And for Thy saving grace;
Hold us, oh Master, ever close,
In Thy divine embrace...

Dear Father, thank Thee for Thy peace,
And for Thy strength and might;
Protect us with Thy gentle hand,
And keep us through the night!

Hope C. Oberhelman

Awaiting Spring's Debut

I await her grand arrival,
Her charm in full array,
And she never disappoints me
Come that lovely month of May.

Her captivating perfume
Will linger on the air,
And babbling brooks and meadows
Will boast her presence there.

The birds up in the treetops
Will serenade the night,
Affording every listening ear
A musical delight.

Beauteous Springtime flowers
Will strike a pleasing pose,
And I'll feel sentimental
As my heart beholds a rose.

Walking through life's garden
On a gorgeous Springtime day
Makes me feel that Heaven
Can't be too far away.

Catherine Janssen Irwin

Forever by My Side

Walk along with me, dear Lord,
    Forever by my side.
Keep me safe from harm, dear Lord,
    Forever be my guide.
Let the flowers bud and bloom
    When springtime fills the air
And let your grace shine down on me
    And eternally be there.
Remain with me throughout my life
    Through every change of season
And never leave my side, dear Lord,
    Not for any reason.

Dolores Karides

Faithful Friend

I was lonely and forsaken
My friends all gone their way,
I ached and felt forgotten
By those I thought would stay.

How sad it is in golden age
Grown old and all alone,
We never thought we'd turn that page,
Life's book was all unknown.

Have you ever felt the quiet
Of a house with no one home,
A threat to future still unmet
Like the calm before the storm?

One day the veil before my eyes
Seemed clearer than before -
A Friend, forgotten, heard my cries
And opened wide the door.

So, worry not about tomorrow
Your faithful Friend is there,
He'll take away all sorrow
And show how much He cares.

I have a Friend, a faithful Friend
Who'll be there till the end
A Friend on whom I can depend,
It's Jesus, who's my Friend.

Toby Munson

But Not
Today

I shall grow old perhaps, but not today,
Not while my hopes are young, my spirit strong,
My vision clear, because life has a way
Of smoothing out the wrinkles with a song.
I shall grow old, perhaps, but not today,
Not while my dreams remain a shining shield,
My faith a lance, and 'neath a sky of grey,
My colors wave upon the battlefield.

I shall grow old, perhaps, but not today,
Not while this pen can write upon a page,
And memories turn Winter into May,
Shall this stout heart be brought to terms by age.
I shall grow old, perhaps, but not today,
And scorning Time who would enlist my tears,
I stand convinced there is a better way,
Of occupying all the coming years.

I shall grow old, perhaps, but not today,
In my own style and in my own sweet time,
No night so dark there does not fall a ray
Of light along the pathway that I climb.
Just say of me, when my last hour slips
Like one bright leaf to softly rest among
The others… "Life was Summer to the heart,
Of one who died believing she was young."

Grace E. Easley

Faith

I care not what tomorrow brings
    Content I am today.
I know the blessed Lord above
    Will hear the words I pray.

I ask Him not for wealth or fame,
    My needs He will provide.
Just give me strength to meet each day,
    Be ever at my side.

He hears my every cry of pain,
    He knows my joys and sorrow.
And He who sees each sparrow's fall
    Will not fail me tomorrow.

Irene Slezak

Heartaches

God can lift the hurt you're feeling,
He can take away each care,
but, you must give Him your burden,
and that's only done through prayer.

God knows everything about you
from beginning to the end,
He can help you like no other,
He's your very dearest friend.

When you're weak He'll make you strong,
when you're sad He brings such peace,
when discouraged He's right with you,
then you feel a sweet release.

He'll walk with you through each valley
till the mountain you ascend,
and it's only through His comfort
that a broken heart can mend.

Don't allow your faith to falter,
don't give up, keep pressing on;
you can make it with the Lord's help,
after darkness comes the dawn.

Shirley McDonald

Voyagers

Upon the sea of life we sail
In ships we build of dreams,
We blindly steer a reckless course,
When charted by our schemes.

We sometimes sail for ports unknown,
When longing to be free,
And like the ancient mariner,
We sail the restless sea.

No port within the storm we find,
No refuge from the gale,
No friendly harbor looms in sight,
As on and on we sail.

But when the Master of the sea
Of life, our ships command,
His loving Hand will lead the way,
To guide us to safe land.

Julie E. Jones

Our Father's Harbor

There's a harbor that lies hidden
In the hearts of all mankind -
And the shoals that guard its entrance,
Are so difficult to find.

Once inside, it is so peaceful -
Breaking waves upon the sand,
Trees that sway from gentle breezes,
Flowers planted by God's hand.

Close your eyes, let your mind wander,
Can't you picture such a place -
It is there for all God's children,
Makes no mind your skin or race.

How to find this hidden harbor,
God will show us all the way,
Let you spirit drift unshackled,
Drop your anchor in this bay.

Then as time on earth grows nigh,
And Jesus reaches down His hand,
He'll lead us to His Father's Harbor,
Many, many times as grand.

Albert N. Theel

Autumn Snow

Daybreak brought a grand surprise
Which so delighted tired eyes -
Upon the hills and all below,
There gleamed a coat of autumn snow!

The crimson leaves were etched in white,
Each a jewel in the morning light.
The aspen gold was covered too
With frozen flakes of morning dew.

Frosted shocks stood row on row
Where corn and pumpkins used to grow.
The meadow showed no trace of green
Where yesterday a fox was seen.

Today the seasons were entwined
To live forever in my mind,
Another gift of God, I know,
Of crimson leaves and autumn snow.

Clay Harrison

Another Day of Life

When the sunrise lights the valley,
The meadows and the hills,
And the birds begin to waken
With their roundelay of trills...
When the whispering of the breezes
Causes flowers to lend an ear,
I waken with rejoicing
And my heart is filled with cheer.

When the dark of night's descending
Over all the countryside,
And the birds all take to roosting,
Having flown their daily flights...
When the stars all dot the heavens
And the moonbeams shed their light,
I give my thanks to God above
For another day of life.

Loise Pinkerton Fritz

Beyond Distress

No longer soft and gentle,
    Wind rushes through the trees
And slips into their shadows
    To twist the withered leaves.

The wind shouts of the winter
    With snow to cabin's eaves
And frost to pattern windows
    With summer's memories.

My body screams arthritis --
    Time's special agonies
Are stiffened, clumsied fingers
    And ancient, creaking knees.

But, still, there's no complaining
    Though lungs must gasp and wheeze --
My appetite is hearty,
    I still do as I please.

In love and understanding
    We have some secret keys
That force life's doors to open
    And show us what God sees.

                Eugene G. E. Botelho

The Log Fire

Far into the winter night,
Adding warmth and cheer,
Our log fire would be burning bright
When frost and snow were here.
Around it, we would chat or sing
Some favorite melody.
While from the kitchen, Mom would bring
Her special cakes and tea.
Later, by our cozy beds,
Before we snuggled in,
Simple evening prayers were said
By lamplight soft and dim.
It was a time of sweet content
In a winter world of white,
That in fellowship was spent
By a log fire burning bright.

Elsie Natalie Brady

Of Thorns and Roses

How beautiful God's roses
    That bloom among the thorns
And scent the Summer breezes
    That play upon the lawn;
A scene - so much akin to life -
    Where virtue is a rose
And thorns of sin await its sway
    To ravage and depose.

Thorns of grief, upon a vine,
    That wait for winds of gale
To drive the rose into their throes -
    To blemish and impale;
As is the same, with thorns of sin
    That wait to pierce our soul
If we should sway - in storms of strife -
    To stray from christian goals.

So, we must guard each rose of life
    Against the thorns of sin
That would deny us Heaven's Grace
    And glories, unto Him,
For life - without its roses
    Of virtue, faith and prayer,
Is just a garden of despair -
    To harvest and to share.

            Michael Dubina

Ribbon of Love

Oh, ribbon of love
From a heart most divine,
Encircling around me
Like diamonds that shine…

Oh, ribbon of love
Fill my heart to the brim,
Erase all the tarnish
Remove all the sin.

Oh, ribbon of love
Cleanse me to see,
That like dew in the morning
You're the prism in me…

Let the blooming continue
Let the harvest be grand,
For I am your prism
And rest in your hand…

Without you I'm nothing
I'm empty and lost,
But you know my true worth,
My soul's actual cost…

So together let's journey
Just one day at a time
For, Lord, I'm your treasure
And "As One"… You are mine…

Chris Zambernard

$\mathcal{I}$ wish you roses
Without the thorns,
Quiet nights
And gentle morn's,
Evening jasmine
And lilac days,
Simple sentences
That heap on praise,
All of this
I wish your way,
Along with Jesus
To bless your day.

James J. Huesgen

Memories

Memories are heartbeats,
Sounding through the years,
Echoes never failing,
Of our smiles and tears.
Moments that are captured,
Sometimes unaware,
Pictures in an album,
Or a lock of hair.

Images that linger
Deep within the mind,
Bits of verse we cherished
Once upon a time.
Through the musty hallways
Of the days we knew,
Ever comes the vision,
Beautiful and true.

Memories are roses
Blooming evermore,
Full of fragrant sweetness,
Never known before.
Life must have a reason,
Goals for which to strive,
Memories are lights that burn
...To keep the heart alive.

Grace E. Easley

I Know

I know there is a sun…
Although the sky is gray,
And even if a storm prevails…
The sun will shine… another day.

I know that there is love and truth…
Although my heart is blue,
For love is there, in all my friends,
and it will come shining through.

I know that God is here with me
In my sorrow and despair
and though I cannot see Him yet
I can feel His loving care.

There is no problem I can't cope with…
No matter how dismal life can be,
Because I know that God, and love and sunshine
Will always be there for me.

I will walk in faith through shadows…
That may surround my sphere,
For I know I do not walk alone…
My God is always near.

Patience Allison Hartbauer

Be not far from me;
for trouble is near;
for there is none to help.
Ps. 22:11

Never Alone

Never alone in the darkness,
Always our Saviour is near,
Comforting us in our sorrow,
Sharing each heartache and tear.

With us in joy and in gladness,
Blessing us from day to day,
Always our constant companion
With us each step of the way.

With us 'tho oft' times we fail Him
Yielding to sin and to pride,
Gracious in mercy, forgiving,
Leading us back to His side.

Never alone for He loves us,
Keeping us safe in His care,
Cheering our heart when discouraged,
Always as close as a prayer.

Sunshine or shadows we've Jesus
And He forsakes not His own;
Walking beside us forever,
Leaving us never alone.

Beverly J. Anderson

Good Morning, Lord

Good morning, Lord, we greet Thee
Protect us through this day.
Grant us wisdom, strength and courage
In all we do - in all we say.

Lord, give us open eyes -
Thy blessings may we see;
And open ears that we may hear
The needs of others where e'er they be.

And wash our thoughts with love,
That steadfastly we'll find
Whatsoever things are good -
To be forgiving, and be kind.

Please walk beside us now,
And with Thy sweet accord,
Stir Thy grace within our beings,
As we say "Good Morning, Lord."

Edna Massimilla

*This is the day which the
Lord hath made; we will
rejoice and be glad in it.*
Psalm 118:24

Omnipotence

Let His goodness be seen
In the mountainous heights,
In the forests and meadows
    And streams;
In the thunderous split
Of the lightening skies,
In soft spaces and places
    To dream.
Let His goodness be seen
In the rose and the thorn,
In the challenge He brings
    At each break of the dawn!
In each song, each prayer,
In each seed of thought
Let His goodness be seen
    And the goodness He wrought!
In the face of a child,
In the eyes of the old...
Let His brightness be seen
    In a radiance bold;
Let His Love be a banner
Unfurled through the years,
And chasing the shadows,
    Erase human fears...
Let His comfort be known
In the solace of words,
Omnipotent God
    Whose voice we have heard!

    Veronica Joan Joslyn

Life is More Worthwhile

If I can help to ease your fears
When you know great distress,
My life will be the more worthwhile
And filled with happiness.

If I can lift your spirits high
By cheerful words I say,
My life will be the more worthwhile
And better every way.

If I can soothe your troubled mind
And help your problems bear,
My life will be the more worthwhile
By helping with you share.

If I can give you faith and hope
And help to ease your pain,
My life will be the more worthwhile
And not one lived in vain.

Harold F. Mohn

As I Go Down the Sunset Hill

As I go down the sunset hill
 I pray, O Lord, that I
Will sweeter and more loving grow
 Until the day I die.
May trouble serve to mellow me,
 And weakness make me kind
To slowness in another's step;
 And let me not be blind
To beauty in the simple things
 That all around me lie,
In people and their loving deeds,
 As well as field and sky.

Oh, make me slow to criticize,
 And quicker to forgive,
And brush away each fancied slight
 As long as I shall live.
Let me take time to savor well
 The good things as I go
Along this sometimes rugged path
 Ablaze with sunset glow.
And may the brightness of Thy love
 Within my heart erase
All earthiness - preparing me
 To look upon Thy face.

Alice Hansche Mortenson

87

*L*ord, thou art God,

which hast made

heaven, and earth,

and the sea, and

all that in them is.

Acts 4:24

Where God Speaks

Some hear the still, small voice of God
    In the song of a meadowlark;
While others claim His voice is heard
    In night sounds after dark.

Others say He speaks to them
    In the whisper of the breeze;
And there are those who hear Him sigh
    In leafy, windblown trees.

But I am one who finds His voice
    In the ocean's stormy roar
Or in the gentler, soothing sound
    As small waves lap the shore.

These sounds are those I love the most
    And so, for a listener like me,
They affirm my loving Master is here
    In the sight and sound of the sea.

Jean Conder Soule

He rose and rebuked
the wind and the
raging of the water:
they ceased and
there was a calm.
Luke 8:24

I Must Pray

When daylight streaks the morning sky
    And I arise to start my day,
To have my heart and mind prepared
    I know so well... that I must pray.

I ask forgiveness for each sin
    As earnestly I start to pray,
That I may put my will aside
    And strive to do His will today.

I thank Him for this brand new day
    And for the night of sleep and rest,
That I might serve Him once again
    My soul and body both refreshed.

I seek His guidance to fulfill
    Whatever task I face today,
So I might be His light of love
    But I am weak... so I must pray.

When shades of night once more foretell
    The ending of another day,
Before I close my eyes in sleep
    I humbly bow... for I must pray.

Gertrude B. McClain

90

Prayer

Are you tired of chasing rainbows,
Walking streets that lead nowhere,
Trying hard but not achieving...
Maybe what you need is prayer.

Is your life so bleak and empty,
Fair weather friends that do not care,
Alone within a crowd of many...
Maybe what you need is prayer.

Our Lord, Jesus, is your answer,
All your problems He will share,
If you'll only bid Him welcome...
Come to Him in solemn prayer.

Suddenly your days are brighter,
You're filled with joy beyond compare,
Now at last you've found the answer...
Since you've come to Him in prayer.

Albert N. Theel

God's Love

With dawn of spring unfolding
    to warm the winter chill
through pasture wood and meadow
    God's love is keeping, still.
On sunlit days of Summer
    when flowers catch the rain
God's love is everflowing
    All nature bears His name.

Upon the close of Summer
    when Autumn comes to pass
God's peace where seeds do slumber
    now lingers 'neath the grass.
When crimson leaves have fallen
    and Winter chills the air
the Holy Birth of Jesus
    all joyfully declare.

But God remains unspoken
    by simple words of rhyme
His love remains unmeasured
    by episodes in time
His peace remains unshaken
    by word-of-mouth or deed
His Word one single flower
    and God Himself the seed.

Thomas P. McHugh

God's Autumn Days

Autumn sings in quiet ways,
When the Cardinals and the Jays
Blend their joyous songs among
Those that human lips have sung.
When the days are crisp and clear,
One can sense that God is near,
Sunlight streaming through the trees,
Brings a body to his knees.

Never has the artist known
Colors like the autumn's own,
Reds and oranges, browns and greys,
Touch the heart in tender ways.
There's a poignant sweetness in
Waters ruffled by the wind,
And the woodsmoke smells of all
Precious things beyond recall.

'Tis a time to pause and rest,
Looking back on worst and best,
Stronger for the wisdom we
Find in each autumn that we see.
And the sunsets all seem golder,
Just as we are growing older,
And the sweetest song life plays,
...Is woven through God's autumn days.

Grace E. Easley

My Dreams Have Wings

My dreams have wings, oh how they fly!
My thoughts are young, my spirits high!
Enthusiasm fills my soul,
With confidence I'll reach my goal!

With an open heart, I spread my wings,
And dare to face what courage brings -
Past troubled waters, stormy seas,
A world of doubt and trembling knees!

Success will come I do believe,
Accomplishments I must achieve,
For I can see no other way,
Just keep on trying - come what may!

My dreams have wings, they grace the sky -
On moonlit nights they multiply,
When summer breezes softly blow,
They fill my heart with inner glow!

Though shadows sometimes cast a spell -
To cause delay - I know so well -
But dark clouds turn to fairest blue -
As soon as sunshine follows through!

The power of prayer can change all things.
It is the force that flies my wings.
A flaming torch, hope is my guide,
As long as Faith is by my side!

Hedwig Wroblewski

Faith

Faith is so very important,
    In the Dear Lord do we trust,
Just imagine how alone we'd be,
    If all we had was us;
Knowing there's someone at our side,
    When the sea of life is rough,
Knowing He'll always be there,
    When the going gets really tough;
Knowing we can count on Him,
    When we fall apart,
Knowing He will care for us,
    With His Sacred Heart;
How comforting it is to have,
    Someone with whom to share,
Our innermost ideas and thoughts,
    To know He's always there;
And that no matter what we do,
    Be it small or great,
He will forever understand,
    And guide us to our fate;
We always have His forgiveness,
    For errors we may make,
Knowing that throughout our life,
    His graces we can take;
So be forever grateful,
    To the Father up above,
For all our prayers He's answered,
    With His undying Love.

Hope Ulch Brown

Harvest Time

Harvest time is praising time
For blessings all year thru,
Our hearts are filled with gratitude
For bounties, not a few.

Our tables all are laden
With delicious things to eat,
Potatoes, corn and biscuits
And cake and pie and meat.

Our wardrobes are so full of clothes
We don't know which to wear,
Our freezers are so full of food
There is no room to spare.

We have vacations every year
And sometimes more than that,
The animals we keep for pets
Are always sleek and fat.

The luxuries we often want
Are sometimes priced quite high,
But all the same they must be ours
We cannot pass them by.

Harvest time is praising time
And time to think of sharing,
A little less of selfishness
A little more of caring.

Lester E. Bartholomew

Thank You, Lord

I love to sit and listen
In the early morning hours
To the buzzing of the busy bees
Taking honey from the flowers.

I love to watch the sunlight
Come filtering through the trees
And hear the happy Meadowlark
Sing songs so merrily.

I love to watch a fluffy cloud
Drift by without a sound.
A butterfly goes dancing by,
A leaf twirls to the ground.

I pause for just a moment;
A silent prayer I say,
"Thank You for my blessings, Lord,
Thank You for this day!"

Mary Ann Houston

It Isn't Home If There's No Love

It isn't love if there's no love -
  It's just a dwelling place,
For home is where the heart ignites
  A smile on every face.

Home is where you rest assured
  That someone really cares,
For here broken hearts are cured
  In answer to your prayers.

Home is where you feel secure
  Because you're not alone,
And you reap a golden harvest
  Of loving seeds you've sown.

Home is your personal oasis
  Where you always quench your thirst,
For those who share it with you
  Will always place you first.

Home's a place to honor God
  And thank Him for His grace...
It isn't home if there's no love -
  It's just a dwelling place.

                    Clay Harrison

Count Your Blessings

Count your blessings, one by one;
    Thank God for every gift --
Reach out to those who are in need,
    And give someone a lift...

Count your blessings, one by one;
    The Lord is by your side,
And He will fill your coffers full,
    Whatever may betide...

Count your blessings, one by one;
    Remember God is love,
And He will touch your heart with peace,
    And guide you from above...

Count your blessings, one by one;
    Rejoice and praise the Lord,
And He will hold you in His hand,
    And give you just reward!

           Hope C. Oberhelman

Thank You, God

We thank You, God, for Springtime,
   For budding, blossoming trees,
For rain that brings growth from the soil,
   For hummingbirds and honey bees.

We thank You for Summer sunshine,
   For white clouds and blue, blue skies,
For wild-flowers blanketing meadows,
   For sunsets to dazzle our eyes.

For bright golden leaves in Autumn,
   For luscious grapes on the vine,
For orchards laden with fruit,
   For Your precious gift of time.

We're thankful for Winter's quiet snow,
   For the caring-love holidays bring,
For Your perfect plan that promises
   Another glorious Spring!

                    Micky Meyer Mathewson

His

His breath whispers in the trees
    With the rustle of each passing breeze;

His art decorates each flower
    With beauty above all human power;

His voice wells up in each song bird
    With clearest melodies ever heard;

His colors adorn each butterfly
    With tints unmatched by any dye;

His hand designs each soft snowflake
    With lines no architect can make;

His might fills sun's golden beams
    With energy beyond our dreams;

His Son shows what true love is;
    With a shepherd's staff He makes us His.

Joseph Hughes Hartough

O' Jesus take each blossom
Blooms in my heart for Thee,
Each one contains a prayer
For my eternity.
May I behold Your face,
All mankind adores,
Behold Your loving heart
From which all blessings pours.

James Joseph Huesgen

The Pathway of Prayer

There is a pathway I walk every day...
It's strewn with flowers of praise,
Praise to our God for His majesty, power,
His goodness and mercy always.
Praise for His glory, His wisdom and truth,
His greatness and excellency;
Praise for His kindness, His pardoning of sin,
His counsel for you and for me.

There is a pathway I walk every day...
It's strewn with flowers of thanks,
Thanks to our God for His infinite love,
His blessings bestowed on all ranks.
Thanks for the gift of His only dear Son
Who triumphed o'er death and the grave;
Thanks be to God for this pathway of prayer
That I might give thanks and praise.

Loise Pinkerton Fritz

Thou wilt show me
the path of life.
Ps. 16:11

Global

Each time we greet
A passer-by
With warm
And friendly smiles,
There is no measuring
The love
That spreads
For unknown miles.

Each little act
of thoughtfulness
To ease
Another's pain,
Sends Charity
From heart to heart
To form
An endless chain.

Each sacrifice
We make for Christ
Though small
Beside the Cross,
Can radiate
God's Grace abroad
And cancel
Any loss.

Amy C. Ellis

Our Promised Land

Sometimes we find it difficult
    to know just what to do:
The map is lost, paths overgrown
    and hidden from our view.
We wander aimlessly along,
    becoming more confused,
Our feet grow tired, and our thoughts
    are harried and bemused.
Which way to turn, what road to take?
    If only we were sure
What lies ahead beyond the bend,
    but vision is obscure.

Oh, foolish mortals that we are
    to let sheer panic grow!
What is to be will be; not ours
    the Master Plan to know.
Slow down a bit, and still the heart
    that trembles with alarm.
It matters not how rough the road,
    we will not come to harm
If we will put our trust in God,
    accept His guiding hand,
Follow His steps; they'll lead us to
    our own true promised land.

Alice J. Christianson

105

The Vigil

My rooms are empty as can be;
no light doth flicker forth for me.
The sun has slipped behind my trees
and dusk brings longing memories.

'Twas long ago, one balmy May,
a family, young, did come to stay;
they patched and painted all my woes,
and trimmed my hedge and gardens hoed.

Time was when all my windows glowed
and lawn and walks did glisten so;
and children's voices echoed round;
and birds sang sweet and pets did bound.

But now no sounds come from within
and silence deafens in my den.
My friends of May, so long ago,
have left, for where I do not know.

Some sorrow have I also known;
of friends that left by death - this home;
young faces, grown, have gone their way;
and I just sit here day by day.

As I remain in lonely rest,
I dream of yesterdays, and yes
of new friends that may come to me;
and light my lamps and help me see.

My role, as given from above,
is comfort and undying love;
and o'er the years I pray to see,
again, old friends once part of me.

William Marshall Weller

Music from God

When God gave us Music, what a glory it was!
From the song of a bird, to the crickets that buzz:

And the low minor wail, of the wind in the trees;
To the symphony sweet, in the hum of the bees.

Oh! yes there is music, in soft summer rain,
As it plays staccato, on your windowpane.

The deep rolling roar of the thundering waves,
Is like the encore of French Horn when it plays.

The soft gurgling brook as it dances along,
Plays light pizzicato or clarinet song.

And thunder claps, in the sky overhead,
Are like crashing cymbals, in symphony led,

By our God, and our Father, Conductor and Friend;
Who gives all His music around us, to bend

Our hearts in submission, in humbleness too.
I'm thankful God gave us Music! Aren't you?

Jeanne Knotts

Jesus Is
the Answer

Jesus is the answer for the world today,
Shining like a lighthouse showing us the way.
Tossed about and shipwrecked on the sea of life
We may find safe harbor, peace 'mid all our strife.

Jesus bids us welcome each and every one.
Matters not who we are or what we have done.
Arms outstretched He's waiting, calling, "Child,
    come home.
There's no need to struggle, out there all alone."

Oh, the blessed comfort for the weary soul,
Resting in the Saviour Whose love makes us whole.
Jesus lifts our burdens giving sweet release,
And our turmoil ceases when He whispers, "Peace."

Anchored safe in Jesus we've no cause to fear.
Pain has turned to gladness with our Lord so near;
And He'll never leave us, faithful Guide is He
Walking close beside us for Eternity.

                    Beverly J. Anderson

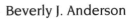

True Love & Joy

The joys of earth all come and go
   Like beauty, in the flowers we grow,
And - like the flowers - their beauty fades
   To memories of different shades;
And so it is with loves and friends -
   Of untrue heart and selfish ends -
Who mark our life with scars of tears
   That mirror heartaches of their years.

But joys and loves that Heaven sends
   Transcend the bonds of earth and friends
And bring us blessings of the Lord
   That grace our life with rich rewards;
And these will never come and go -
   As fonds and frills the earth bestows -
For they are gifts for us to keep
   And share and sow - to further reap.

So let us not bemoan despairs
   Of joys and loves that life impairs
But glory in the gifts of love
   That God endears us, from above,
And find - in Him - true love and joy
   That life and strife cannot destroy;
And find - in Him - the friend we need
   To share, with us, our life and creed.

Michael Dubina

Optimistic

Nature is an optimist
   The sun sinks in the west
To rise again in glorious dawn
   And prove that God knows best!

Nature is an optimist
   For when the dark clouds cry
You often see the rainbow's hues
   Arched across the sky.

Nature is an optimist
   Rejoicing in new birth
And bird songs fill the fresh new air
   As spring returns to earth.

Nature is an optimist
   Behold the message plain
In frosty white, etched tropic plants
   On winter's windowpane.

Nature is an optimist
   According to God's plan
Each follows its own destiny
   Lord help me that I can!

Nature is an optimist
   And as I'm growing old
God gives me hope of greater things
   New Life of joys untold.

May I, too, be an optimist
   I know day follows night
What is not mine to understand,
   Needs faith, God makes it right!

Eva Braswell

The Changing of the Guard

For just a fleeting instant, when,
The nighttime greets the dawn,
A hushed expectancy awaits,
With bated breath, indrawn.

An amber sun lights jeweled webs,
That nighttime weavers spun,
And cricket symphonies are stilled,
A new song has begun.

From trees, a trilling melody,
Awakens all around,
The distant valleys, wooded hills,
Echo the joyous sound.

A waning moon and scattered stars,
So quickly pass from view,
The changing of the guard has wrought,
A glorious day that's new.

Julie E. Jones

Teach Me, Lord

Lord deliver me from thinking
That I am always right.
Keep me from saying hurting things
To everyone in sight.
Impress upon me deeply,
I am not "one-of-a-kind,"
That mirrors lie as well as lips,
And sometimes eyes are blind.

Don't let me for an instant think
I'm better than the rest,
It's what is deep within my heart,
And not how I am dressed.
It's how I live, not where I live,
That matters in the end,
It isn't who I know or all
The places I have been.

It's sharing and it's caring,
And it's finding time to be
As tolerant of others, Lord,
As You have been with me.
For Life is short, and Death is sure,
And then Eternity...
Lord, teach me how to be a friend,
...And not a pharisee.

Grace E. Easley

Reach Out

Reach out and take our Saviour's hand
    It's such an easy thing to do
You will find that you can trust Him
    He will always see you through.

You can lean on Him when you need to
    He will never allow you to fall
He's closer than your next heartbeat
    He'll hear your slightest call.

If you cannot walk, He'll carry you
    Until you're able to travel again;
The peace and the joy He'll give all the while
    Is beyond the understanding of men.

So reach out and take our Saviour's hand
    You've all to gain and naught to lose
He's waiting and bids you come to Him,
    But it's up to you to choose.

Darlene R. Fountain

My Refuge And My Strength

God is my refuge and my strength
When failure comes my way.
He gives me hope and strength anew
To face each new born day.

He is my inspiration
In all I strive to do,
And is the light that guides me
Each day my whole life through.

How barren and how hopeless
This life of mine would be,
If God were not a part of it
Within the heart of me.

Harold F. Mohn

My Own
Gethsemane

I shall not bow to pain or sorrow,
but rather - take what comes tomorrow.
　I will accept what Thou must give,
and thank Thee for each day I live.

　My cross grows heavy now and then,
but - my thoughts go back to when
　Thou carried Thine, and died for me,
and God, I'd do the same for Thee!

　So send me crosses at Thy will.
Then, please help me climb each hill,
　for without Thee no strength is mine,
and every hill too steep to climb.
　Stay by my side - that I may be
prepared for my Gethsemane!

Doris A. Orth

With Praise,
Reaching Up

Jesus within me
has given me eyes -
Eyes to see beauty
where true beauty lies.
Ears to hear small sounds -
a bird in a tree;
The whisper of someone
that's speaking to me.
A nose to smell fragrance -
a flower in bloom,
A breeze lifting cool air
into a warm room.
The taste of an apple,
or fruit from the vine,
Sweet cider or grape juice
as fine vintage wine.
Hands to write letters
and do for my friends;
The earth spread around me...
the joy never ends.
A voice to recite what
the Lord bids me say,
And feet, where the Spirit of God
shows the way.

Yes, Jesus within me,
the day will disclose:
I'm happy and thankful,
the dear Father knows.

Roxie Lusk Smith

Do Them Now

If you think kind thoughts about me,
Won't you please tell me today.
Cause unless you guard it carefully,
Tomorrow it may slip away.

If you're longing to help me,
Just go ahead I pray,
For who knows in the morning,
I may have flown away.

If you need to forgive me,
Make haste and don't delay.
For it won't bring me gladness,
When I'm sleeping 'neath the clay.

Let us hurry, time is wasting,
Soon the opportunity is past.
And we stand before the Father,
It's too late, we find at last.

Let us spend every moment,
Doing everything we can.
Then there'll be no tears of sorrow,
When before the Lord we stand.

Dottlee Duggan Reid

Morning Prayer

In the quiet of God's presence,
    We welcome this new day.
We humbly pray for guidance -
    Keep us on the narrow way.

Help us do for others -
    Greet them with a smile,
Lend a helping hand,
    And walk that extra mile.

Grant us an inner peace,
    That only You can give -
A serenity that will last
    So long as we shall live.

Then when the day is ended -
    Cares all laid aside,
We'll give God all the glory -
    Our Master and our Guide.

Erma Fajen MacFarlane

*W*ere you too busy this morning
    to quietly stop and pray -
Did you hurry and drink you coffee
    then frantically rush away?
Consoling yourself by saying,
    "God will always be there -
Waiting to hear my petitions
    ready to answer each prayer"
It's true the great generous Savior
    forgives our transgressions each day
And patiently waits for lost sheep
    who constantly seem to stray -
But moments of prayer once omitted
    in the busy rush of the day
Can never again be recaptured
    for they silently slip away.
So seek the Lord in the morning
    and never forget Him at night
For prayer is an unfailing blessing
    that makes every burden seem light.

Helen Steiner Rice

Used with permission of
The Helen Steiner Rice Foundation
Cincinnati, OH 45202

Friendly Invite

That phone call is a blessing when
    A friend is ringing you
And asks if there is anything
    You really have to do.
Or do you have the time to spare
    To spend an evening gay
With relaxation truly good
    To help you on your way?
It is the phone call wonderful
    That is a nice surprise,
Just when you are too tired to
    Get up and exercise.
And that is when it really pays
    To have that friend so true,
Who really loves you and who wants
    To be of help to you.
That phone call is so marvelous
    Just when you need it most,
It makes you deeply grateful to
    Your gracious, timely host.

James J. Metcalfe

121

Love and Mercy

Let the warmth of your love
melt the ice in your heart,
So forgive and forget
and make a new start,
For anger and hate
harms the one who recalls
the sins made against him
and builds up high walls.
Don't lock yourself up
in a place full of hate,
Forgive and forget
before it's too late.
Let mercy and love
play a role in your life,
To free you from discord
and the perils of strife.
Then peace, joy and hope
will enter your soul,
And loving compassion
will make your life whole.

Dolores Karides

When you pray,
forgive if you have
anything against
another; that your
Father in heaven
may forgive you.
Mark 11:25

122

Church Bells

This old world is full of sadness,
And it seems no one's immune.
There is so much of madness,
And people out of tune,
But I'll tell you what I've noticed,
It's a soothing sort of thing,
If you'll just relax and listen,
When you hear the church bells ring.

You may not be well in body,
And it seems that's oft' the case,
You may have some circumstances,
Which you feel you cannot face,
And even though your pocketbook,
Will not produce a dime,
You will feel a little better,
When you hear the church bells chime.

When you end your days of labor,
And you've no more trials to face,
You will go to meet your loved ones,
Who've outstripped you in the race,
I am sure you'll feel 'twas worth it,
To have served the Lord with zeal,
Just to hear the Father's "welcome,"
As the bells of Heaven peal.

Lester E. Bartholomew

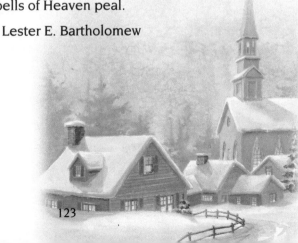

I Do Not Look
Beyond Today

I do not look beyond today
To what the future has in store,
I give each moment, one by one
To Him and ask, He go before.

Yes, I must take but just one day
That is enough for me to do,
And with God walking by my side
His hand in mine we'll see it through.

And though the day be dark or bright,
If I have God to be my guide,
I know that I can trust in Him
And all my needs will be supplied.

He helps me as I do each task
He hears each prayer that I have said,
I sing to Him my praises sweet,
'Tis by His word that I am fed.

I know He is my life, my all
He bore the cross to Calvary
For me it bought redemption, thus
He shed His blood and now I'm free.

I do not look beyond today
To what the future has in store
I trust unto His guiding hand
To lead me safely to the shore.

Mary E. Herrington

The Angelus

The angelus is ringing,
High upon the hill,
Emitting thoughts of His love,
Proclaiming, that He will,
Ever be, your constant guide,
through the trials you bear,
Removing doubt and worry,
With His loving care.

The angelus is ringing,
High upon the hill,
Ringing forth another day,
To fulfill His will,
In every thought and action,
He will be your guide,
With truth and love, He'll lead you,
Remaining by your side.

The angelus is ringing,
High upon the hill,
Assuring with each new born day,
That He loves you still.
So give thanks, to Him who cares,
In whom, you can confide,
Knowing that, eternally,
He will, with you abide.

Colette Fedor

Prayer for the Animals

Lord, watch the rabbit with his hop,
The squirrel eating apple cores,
Protect the cats that cross the streets,
The little dogs that scratch our doors.

Look down on deer within the woods,
And mice in dusty corners, too,
For all of them make picture books
To children with the things they do --

I know that animals can't pray,
So I implore you, God, to keep
Your watchful eye on them each day,
Your angel guard while they're asleep!

Marion Schoeberlein

The Seasons of Life

Seasons come and go away,
Nothing remains the same,
Our dreams and heartfelt wishes,
Seem but a weary game.

Our life is like a vapour,
As it quickly slips away,
And all that's left are memories
Of some other happy day.

It seems that only yesterday
I was in the springtime of life,
Now the winter is approaching,
With its aging and its strife.

The harvestime has ended,
The summer has come and gone,
The seasons of life keep changing,
As the cycle hurries on.

I am looking for a future time
When all the seasons will be one,
It will be a sinless, ageless, paradise,
In the presence of God and His Son.

Frances Culp Wolfe

*To everything there
is a season, and a
time to every purpose.*
Eccl. 3:1

Footprints

Footprints in the sand,
Footprints in the snow --
Our tracks we leave behind
Wherever we may go.

Ev'ry trail we make
Other souls can see,
And, choosing roads to take,
May follow you and me.

May the road we tread
Please our God above,
That others might be led
In paths of truth and love.

Footprints in the sand,
Footprints in the snow --
If led by God's own hand,
His way of love we'll show.

Kathryn Thorne Bowsher